POP HITS

HAL•LEONARD MANDOLIN PLAY-ALONG

VOL. 3

Mandolin by Mike Cramer

ISBN 978-1-4584-1387-1

T0039767

HAL•LEONARD®
CORPORATION
7777 W. BLUEMOUND RD. P.O. BOX 13819 MILWAUKEE, WI 53213

Brown Eyed Girl

Words and Music by Van Morrison

Intro
Moderately fast ♩ = 146

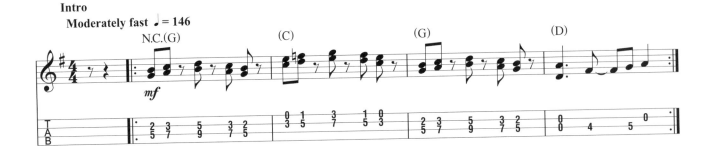

Verse

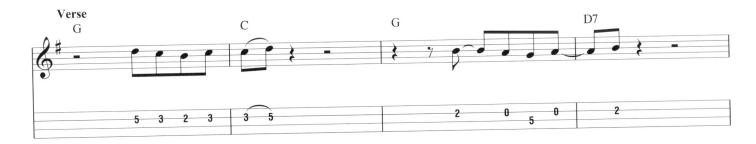

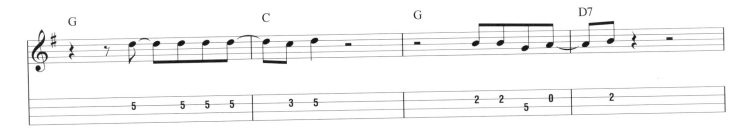

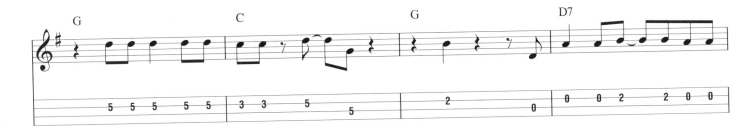

Verse

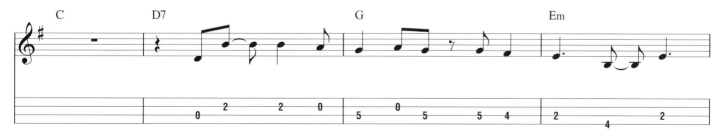

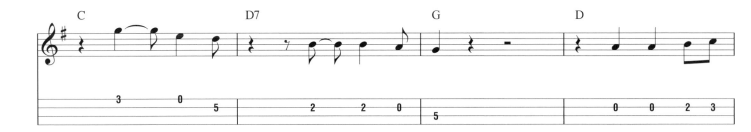

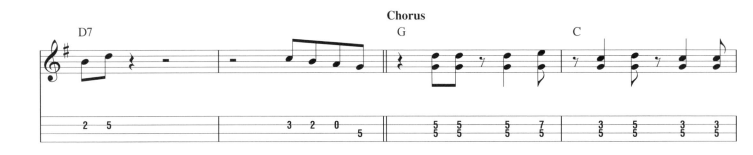

Chorus

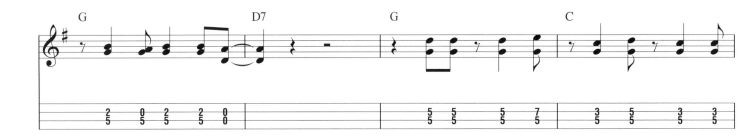

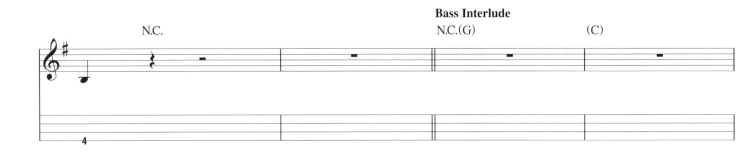

Bass Interlude

Verse

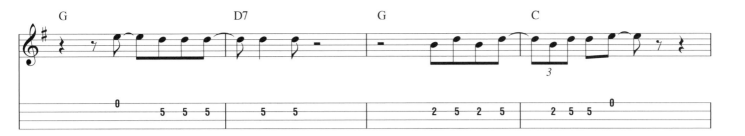

Outro-Chorus

Repeat and fade

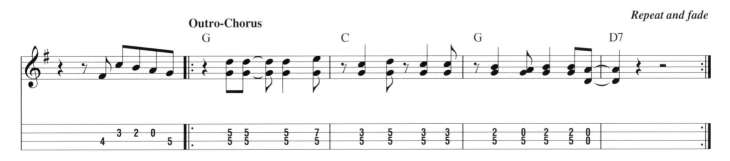

I Shot the Sheriff

Words and Music by Bob Marley

TRACK 3

Chorus

Moderately slow Reggae ♩ = 94

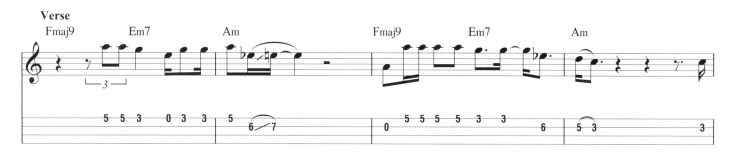

Verse

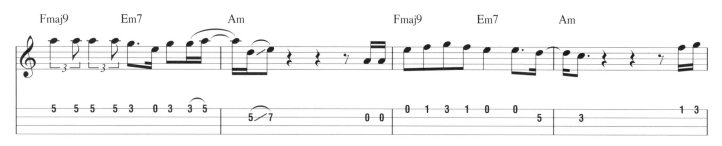

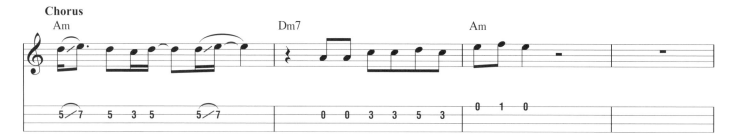

Chorus

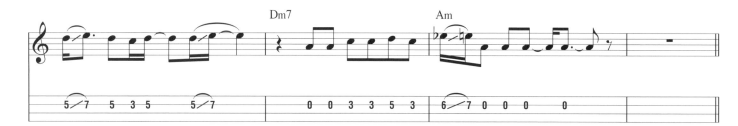

Verse

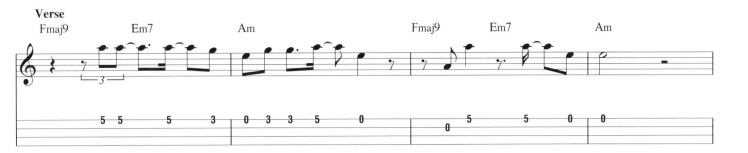

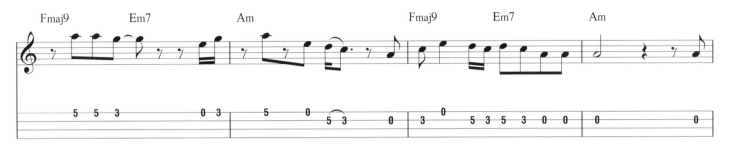

Chorus

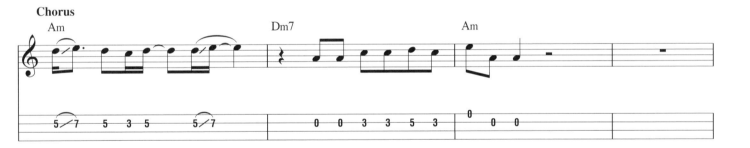

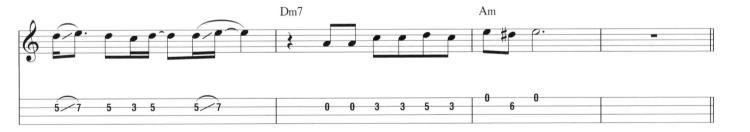

Verse

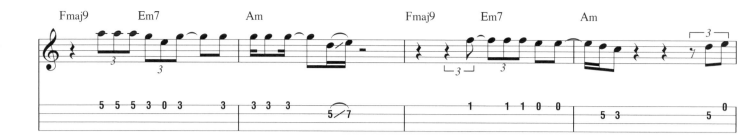

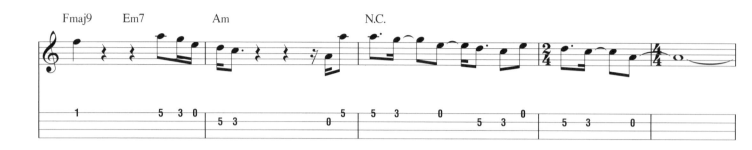

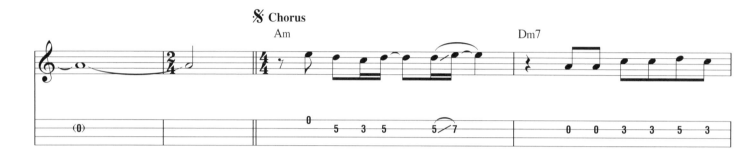

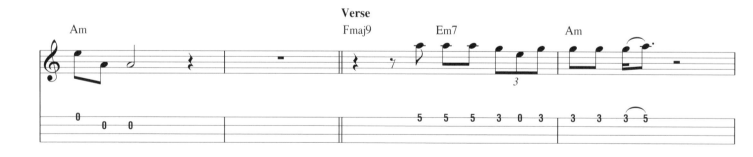

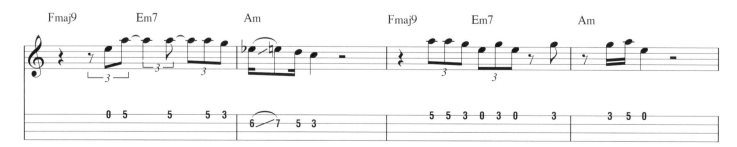

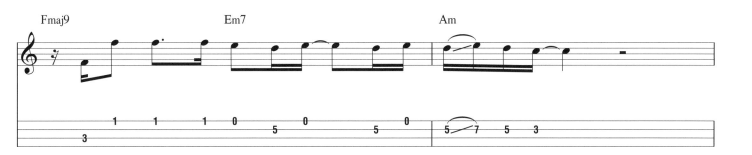

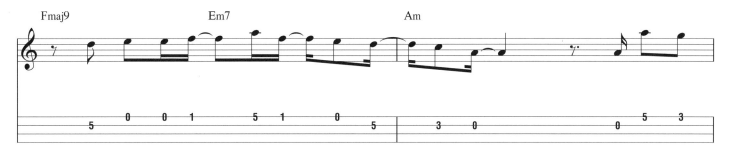

D.S. al Coda

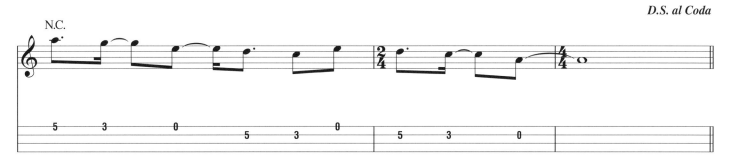

Coda

Outro

Repeat and fade

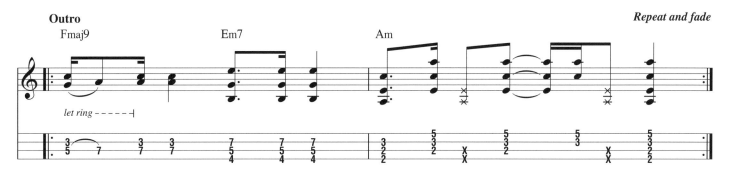

In My Life

Words and Music by John Lennon and Paul McCartney

Intro

Moderately ♩ = 104

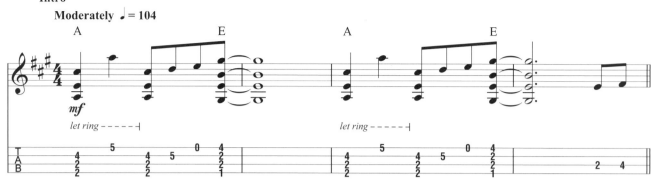

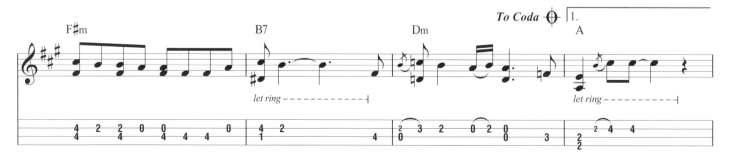

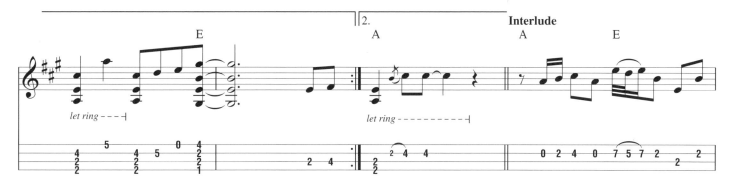

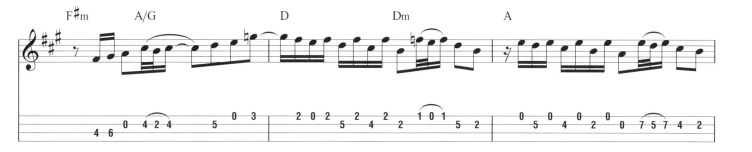

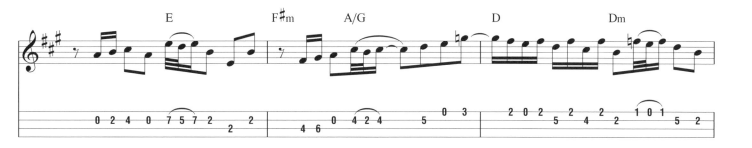

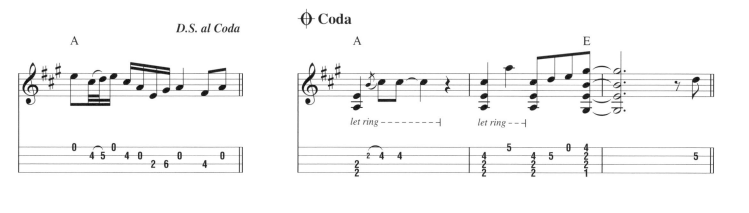

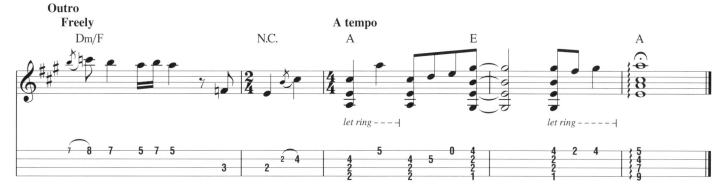

TRACK 7

Mrs. Robinson
Words and Music by Paul Simon

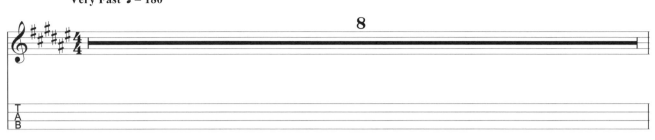

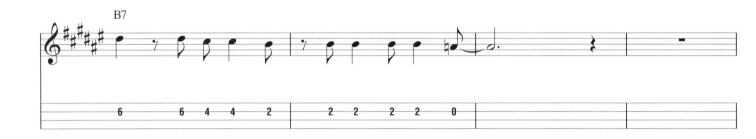

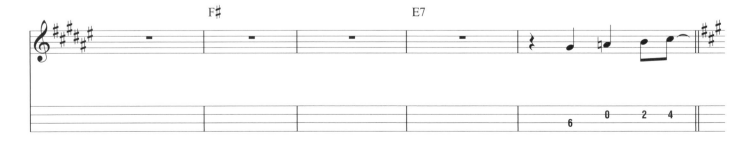

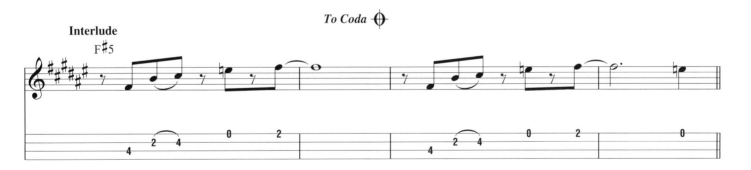

14

Interlude

Verse

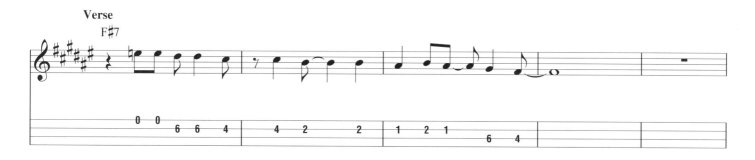

D.S. al Coda

Coda

Verse

Chorus

Outro

Repeat and fade

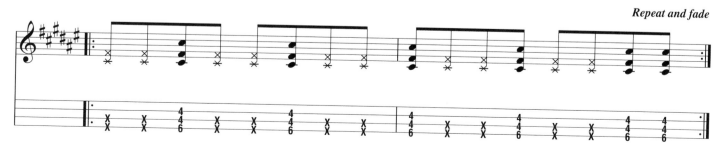

Stand by Me

Words and Music by Jerry Leiber, Mike Stoller and Ben E. King

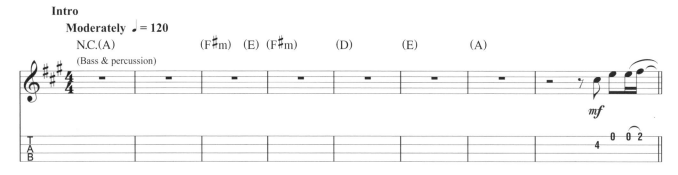

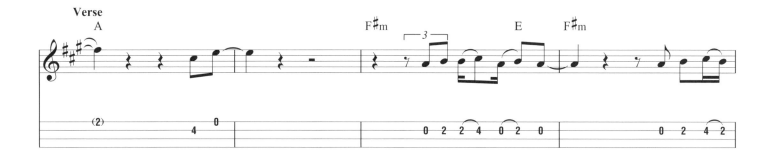

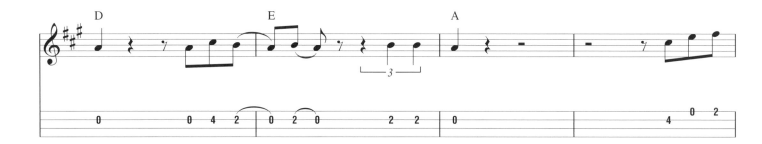

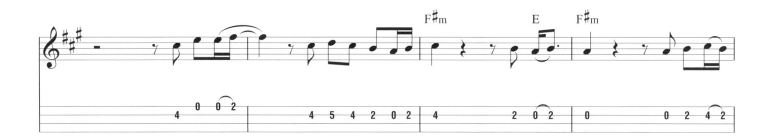

Chorus

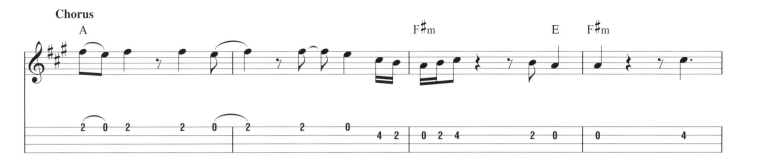

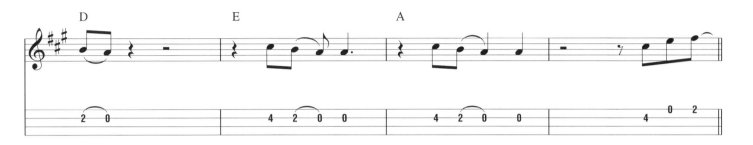

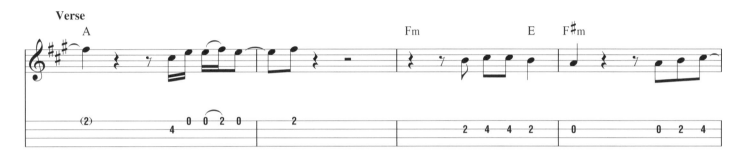

Verse

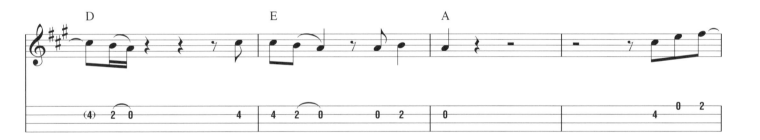

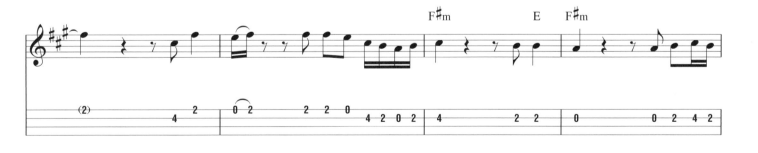

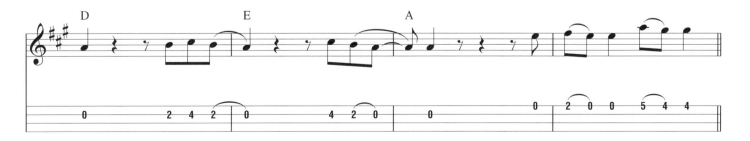

Chorus

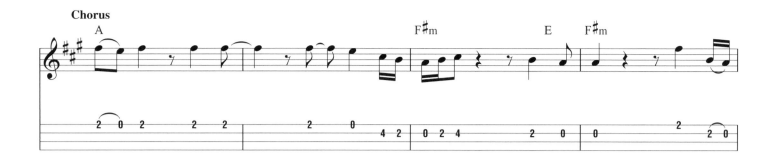

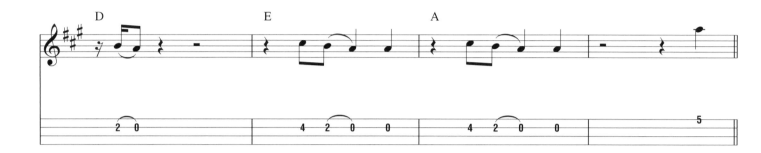

Interlude

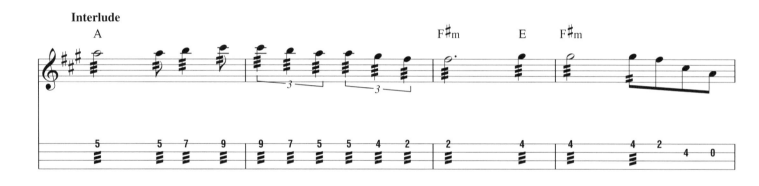

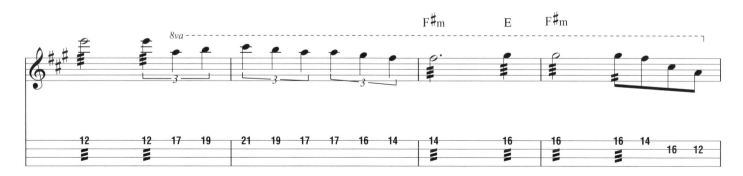

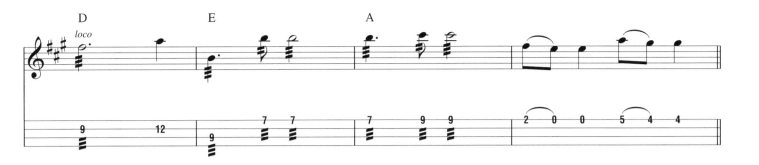

Outro-Chorus

Begin fade

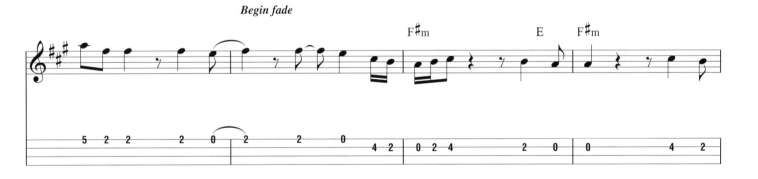

Fade out

Superstition

Words and Music by Stevie Wonder

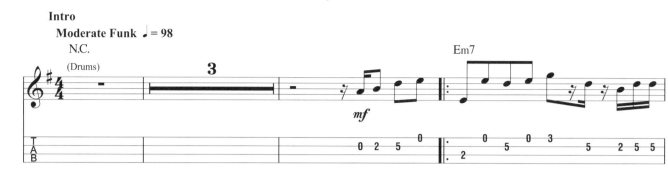

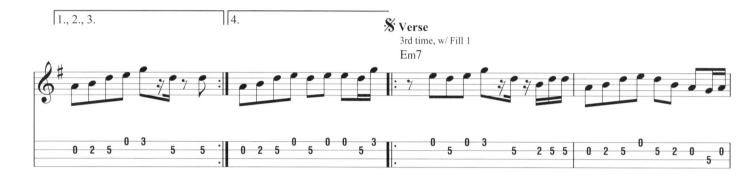

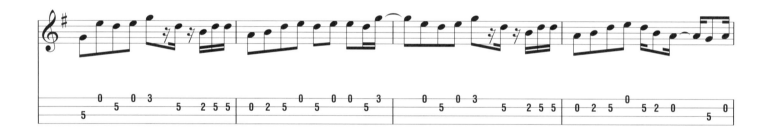

Chorus

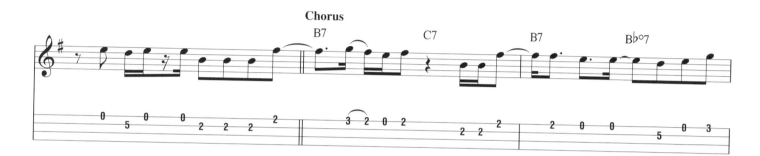

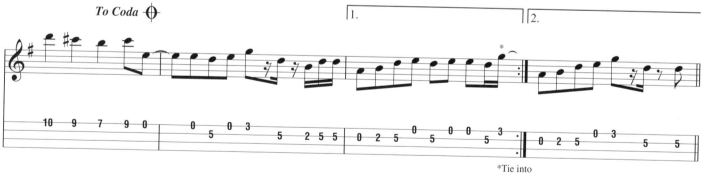

*Tie into
beat one.

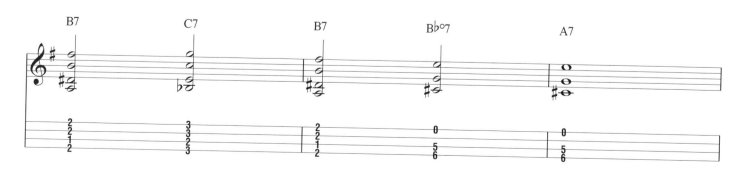

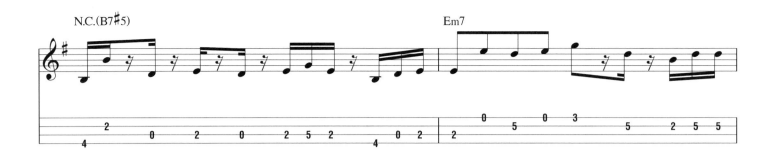

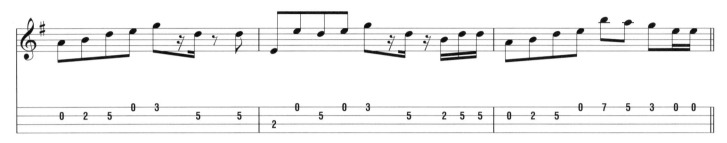

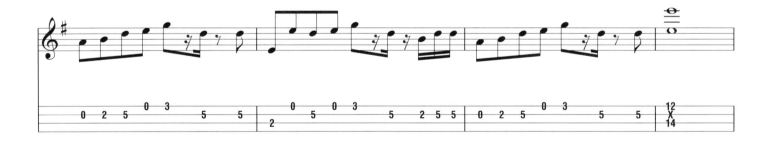

Tears in Heaven

Words and Music by Eric Clapton and Will Jennings

Intro

Moderately slow ♩ = 80

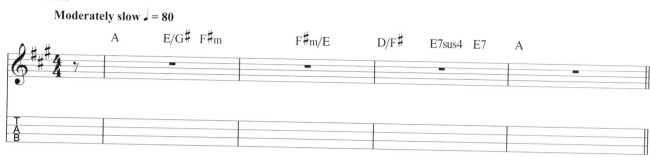

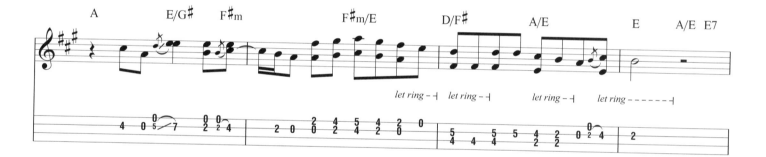

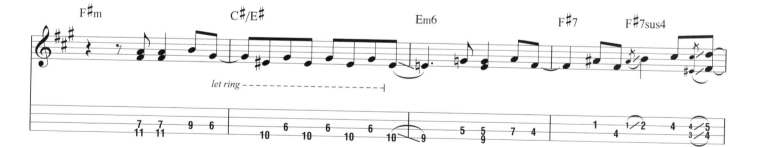

To Coda

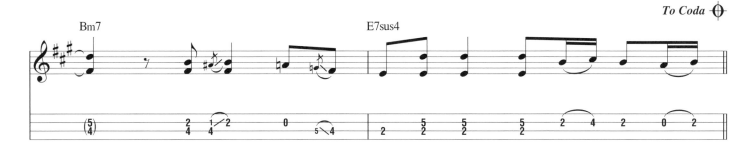

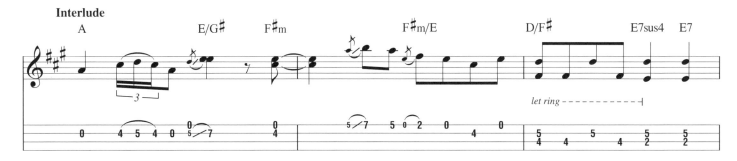

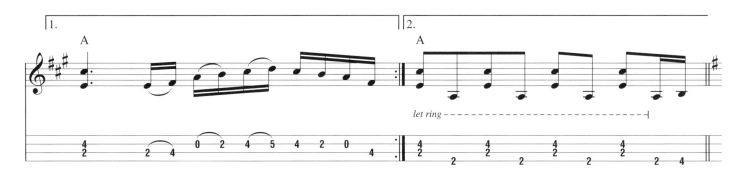

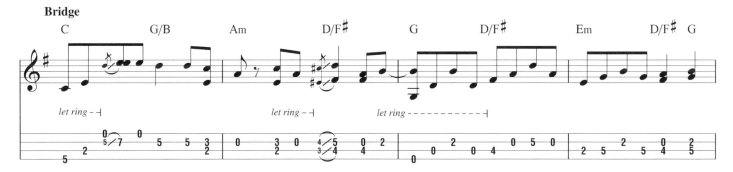

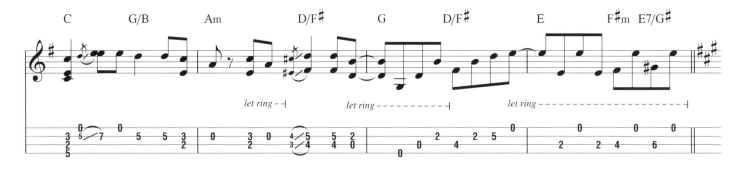

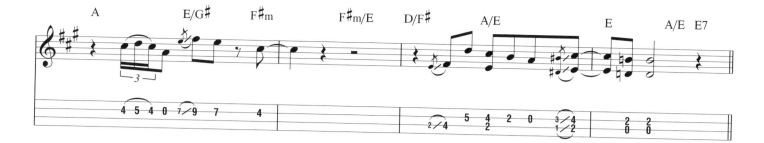

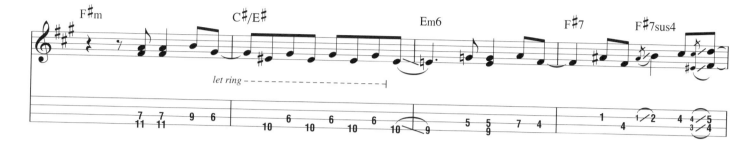

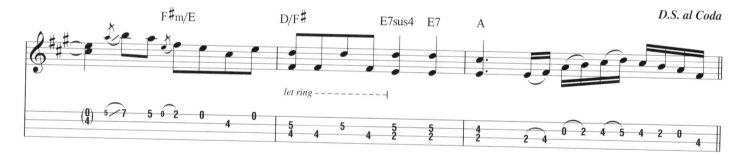

⊕ Coda

Outro

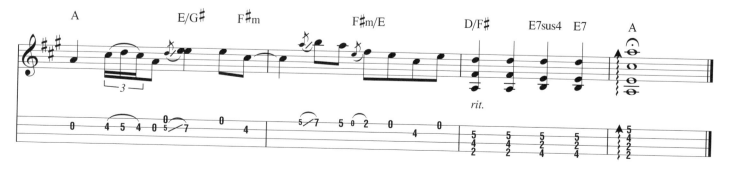

You Can't Hurry Love

Words and Music by Edward Holland, Lamont Dozier and Brian Holland

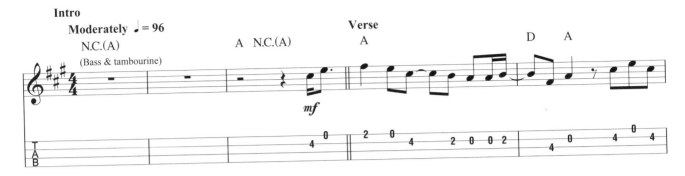

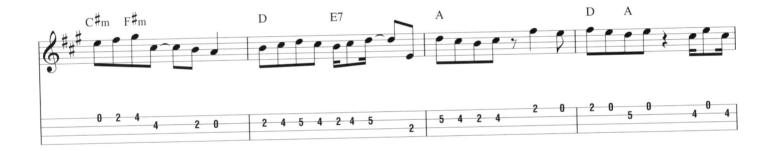

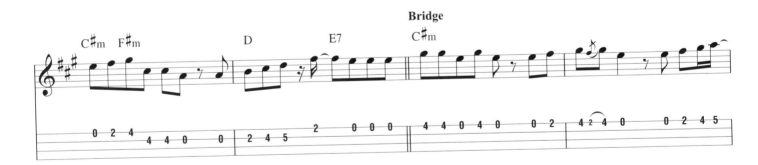

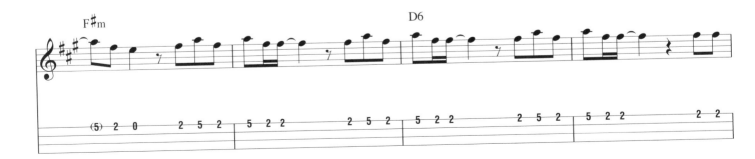

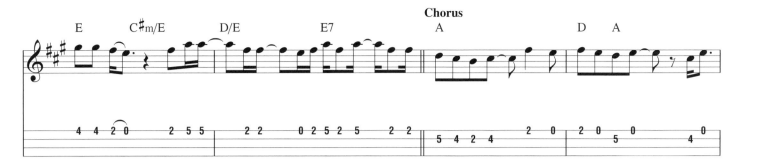

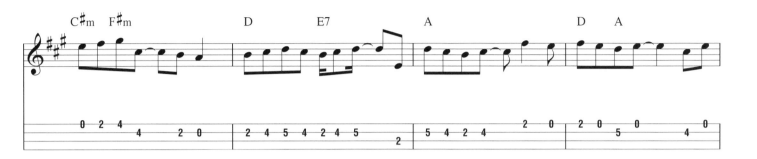

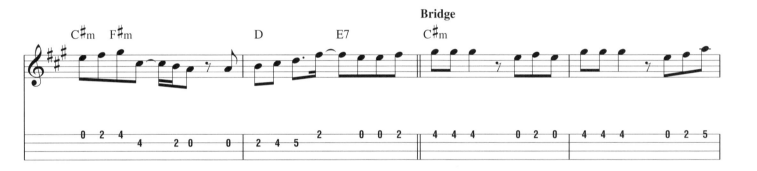

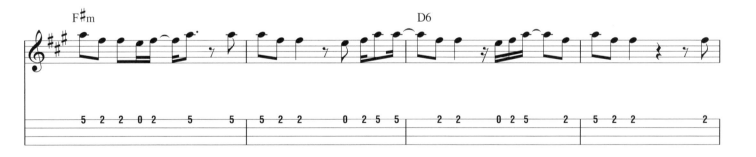

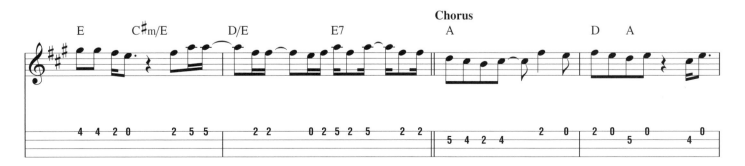

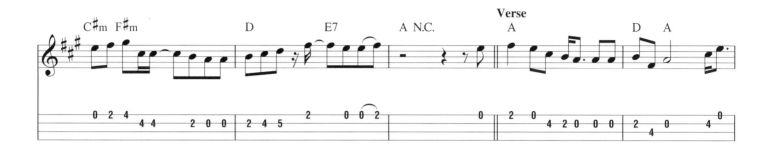

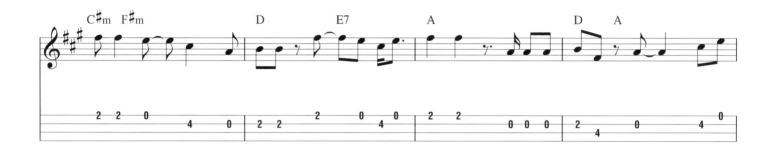

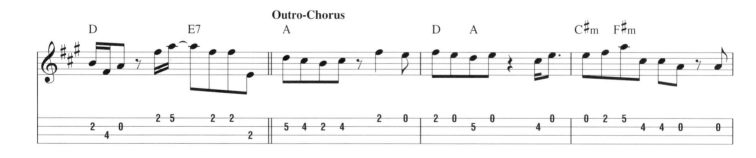

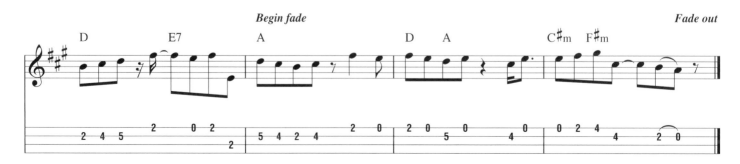

MANDOLIN NOTATION LEGEND

Mandolin music can be notated three different ways: on a *musical staff,* in *tablature,* and in *rhythm slashes.*

RHYTHM SLASHES are written above the staff. Strum chords in the rhythm indicated. Use the chord diagrams found at the top of the first page of the transcription for the appropriate chord voicings.

THE MUSICAL STAFF shows pitches and rhythms and is divided by bar lines into measures. Pitches are named after the first seven letters of the alphabet.

TABLATURE graphically represents the mandolin fretboard. Each of the four horizontal lines represents each of the four courses of strings, and each number represents a fret.

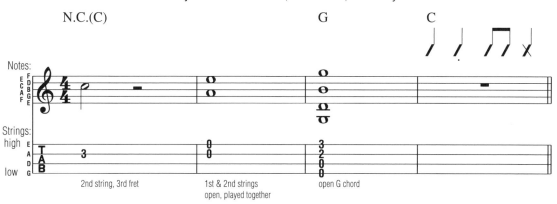

2nd string, 3rd fret   1st & 2nd strings open, played together   open G chord

Definitions for Special Mandolin Notation

MUTED STRING(S): Lightly touch a string with the edge of your fret-hand finger while fretting a note on an adjacent string, causing the muted string to be unheard. Muting all of the strings with the fingers of the fret-hand while strumming the strings with the picking hand produces a percussive effect.

HAMMER-ON: Strike the first (lower) note with one finger, then sound the higher note (on the same string) with another finger by fretting it without picking.

PULL-OFF: Place both fingers on the notes to be sounded. Strike the first note and, without picking, pull the finger off to sound the second (lower) note.

LEGATO SLIDE: Strike the first note and then slide the same fret-hand finger up or down to the second note. The second note is not struck.

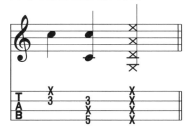

SHIFT SLIDE: Same as the legato slide except the second note is struck.

HALF-STEP BEND: Strike the note and bend up ½ step.

GRACE NOTE BEND: Strike the note and immediately bend up as indicated.

TREMOLO PICKING: The note is picked rapidly and continuously.

Additional Musical Definitions

p (piano) • Play quietly.

mp (mezzo-piano) • Play moderately quiet.

mf (mezzo-forte) • Play moderately loud.

f (forte) • Play loudly.

cont. rhy. sim. • Continue strumming in similar rhythm.

N.C. (no chord) • Don't strum until the next chord symbol. Chord symbols in parentheses reflect implied harmony.

D.S. al Coda • Go back to the sign (𝄋), then play until the measure marked *"To Coda,"* then skip to the section labeled **"Coda."**

D.S.S. al Coda 2 • Go back to the double sign (𝄋𝄋), then play until the measure marked *"To Coda 2",* then skip to the section labeled **"Coda 2."**

D.S. al Fine • Go back to the sign (𝄋), then play until the label *"Fine."*

(staccato) • Play the note or chord short.

rit. *(ritard)* • Gradually slow down.

(fermata) • Hold the note or chord for an undetermined amount of time.

• Repeat measures between signs.

1. 2. • When a repeated section has different endings, play the first ending only the first time and the second ending only the second time.

NOTE: Tablature numbers in parentheses mean:
1. The note is being sustained over a system (note in standard notation is tied), or
2. The note is sustained, but a new articulation (such as a hammer-on, pull-off or slide) begins.

Great Mandolin Publications

from

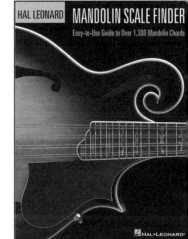

HAL•LEONARD®

HAL LEONARD MANDOLIN METHOD
INCLUDES TAB

Noted mandolinist and teacher Rich Del Grosso has authored this excellent mandolin method that features great playable tunes in several styles (bluegrass, country, folk, blues) in standard music notation and tablature. The optional audio features play-along duets.
00699296 Book Only $7.99
00695102 Book/CD Pack $15.99

EASY SONGS FOR MANDOLIN
SUPPLEMENTARY SONGBOOK TO THE HAL LEONARD MANDOLIN METHOD

20 songs to play as you learn mandolin: Annie's Song • California Dreamin' • Let It Be • Puff the Magic Dragon • Scarborough Fair • Where Have All the Flowers Gone? • and more.
00695865 Book Only $7.99
00695866 Book/CD Pack $15.99

FRETBOARD ROADMAPS – MANDOLIN
INCLUDES TAB
THE ESSENTIAL PATTERNS THAT ALL THE PROS KNOW AND USE
by Fred Sokolow and Bob Applebaum
The latest installment in our popular Fretboard Roadmaps series is a unique book/CD pack for all mandolin players. The CD includes 48 demonstration tracks for the exercises that will teach players to: play all over the fretboard, in any key; increase their chord, scale and lick vocabulary; play chord-based licks, moveable major and blues scales, first-position major scales and double stops; and more! Includes easy-to-follow diagrams and instructions for all levels of players.
00695357 Book/CD Pack $12.95

MANDOLIN CHORD FINDER
EASY-TO-USE GUIDE TO OVER 1,000 MANDOLIN CHORDS
BY CHAD JOHNSON

Learn to play chords on the mandolin with this comprehensive, yet easy-to-use book. The Hal Leonard Mandolin Chord Finder contains over 1,000 chord diagrams for the most important 28 chord types, including three voicings for each chord. Also includes a lesson on chord construction, and a fingerboard chart of the mandolin neck!
00695739 9" X 12" Edition $6.95
00695740 6" X 9" Edition $5.99

MANDOLIN SCALE FINDER
EASY-TO-USE GUIDE TO OVER 1,300 MANDOLIN SCALES
by Chad Johnson
Presents scale diagrams for the most often-used scales and modes in an orderly and easily accessible fashion. Use this book as a reference guide or as the foundation for creating an in-depth practice routine. Includes multiple patterns for each scale, a lesson on scale construction, and a fingerboard chart of the mandolin neck.
00695779 9" X 12" Edition $6.95
00695782 6" X 9" Edition $5.95

BILL MONROE – 16 GEMS
INCLUDES TAB

Authentic mandolin transcriptions of these classics by the Father of Bluegrass: Blue Grass Breakdown • Blue Grass Special • Can't You Hear Me Calling • Goodbye Old Pal • Heavy Traffic Ahead • I'm Going Back to Old Kentucky • It's Mighty Dark to Travel • Kentucky Waltz • Nobody Loves Me • Old Crossroad Is Waitin' • Remember the Cross • Shine Hallelujah Shine • Summertime Is Past and Gone • Sweetheart You Done Me Wrong • Travelin' This Lonesome Road • True Life Blues.
00690310 Mandolin Transcriptions $12.95

O BROTHER, WHERE ART THOU?
INCLUDES TAB

Perfect for beginning to advanced players, this collection contains both note-for-note transcribed mandolin solos, as well as mandolin arrangements of the melody lines for 11 songs from this Grammy-winning Album of the Year: Angel Band • The Big Rock Candy Mountain • Down to the River to Pray • I Am a Man of Constant Sorrow • I Am Weary (Let Me Rest) • I'll Fly Away • In the Highways (I'll Be Somewhere Working for My Lord) • In the Jailhouse Now • Indian War Whoop • Keep on the Sunny Side • You Are My Sunshine. Chord diagrams provided for each song match the chords from the original recording, and all songs are in their original key. Includes tab, lyrics and a mandolin notation legend.
00695762 .... $12.99

THE ULTIMATE BLUEGRASS MANDOLIN CONSTRUCTION MANUAL
by Roger H. Siminoff
This is the most complete step-by-step treatise ever written on building an acoustical string instrument. Siminoff, a renowned author and luthier, applies over four decades of experience to guide beginners to pros through detailed chapters on wood selection, cutting, carving, shaping, assembly, inlays, fretting, binding and assembly of an F-style mandolin.
00331088 .... $34.95

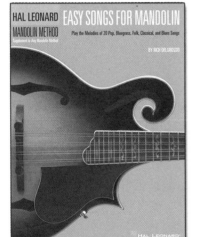

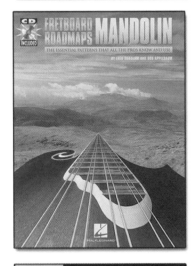

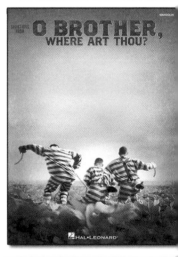

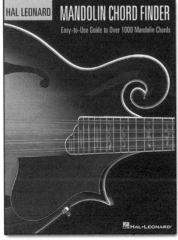

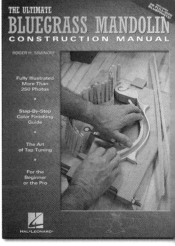

Prices, contents and availability are subject to change without notice.